SKETCHBOOK FOR KIDS

Jan Alexander Quintos

To order additional copies of this book, contact:
Xlibris
1-888-795-4274
www.Xlibris.com
Orders@Xlibris.com

ISBN: Softcover   978-1-7960-6268-7
         EBook   978-1-7960-6267-0

Print information available on the last page

Rev. date: 09/27/2019

SKETCHBOOK
FOR KIDS

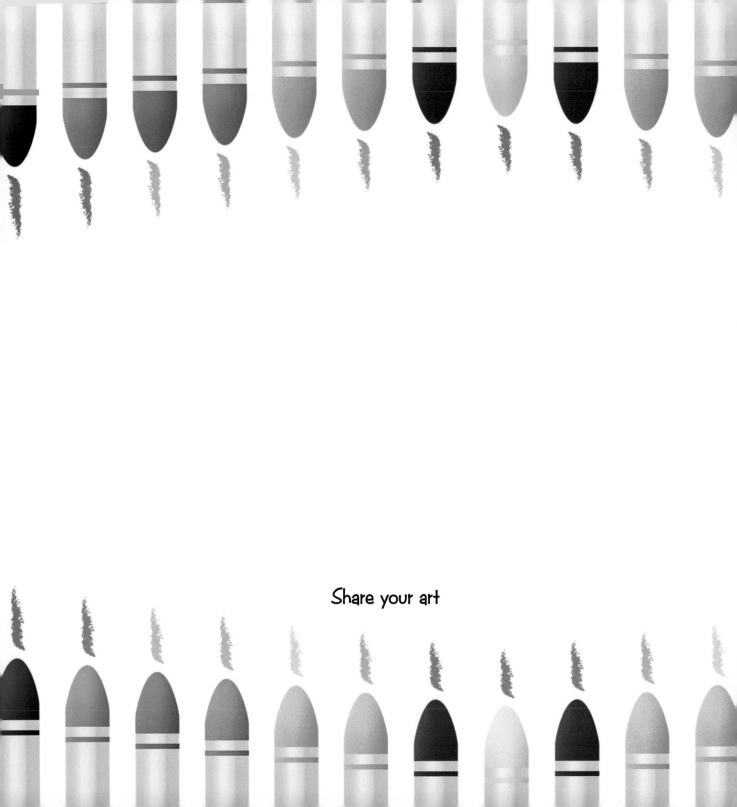

Share your art

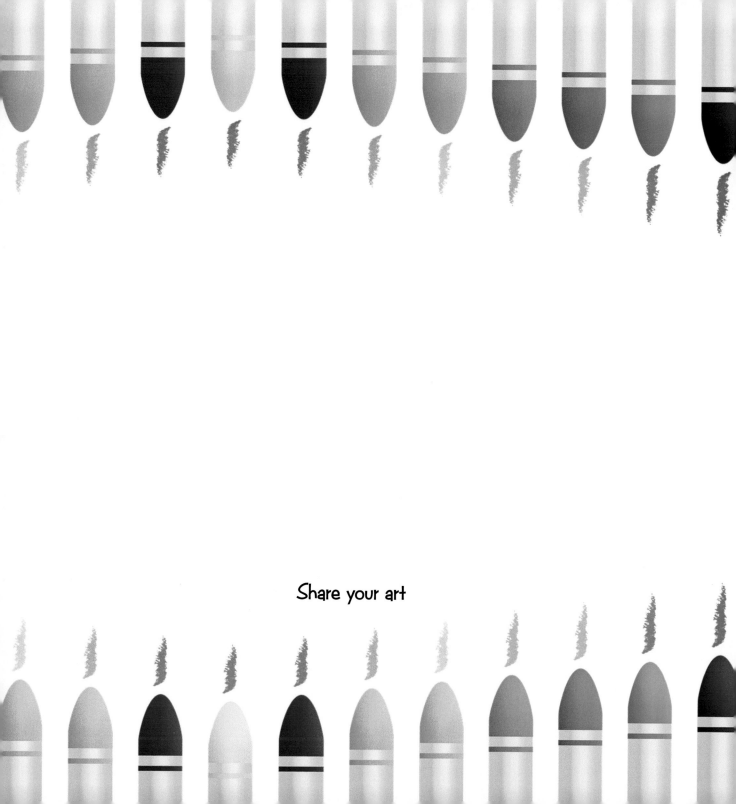

Share your art

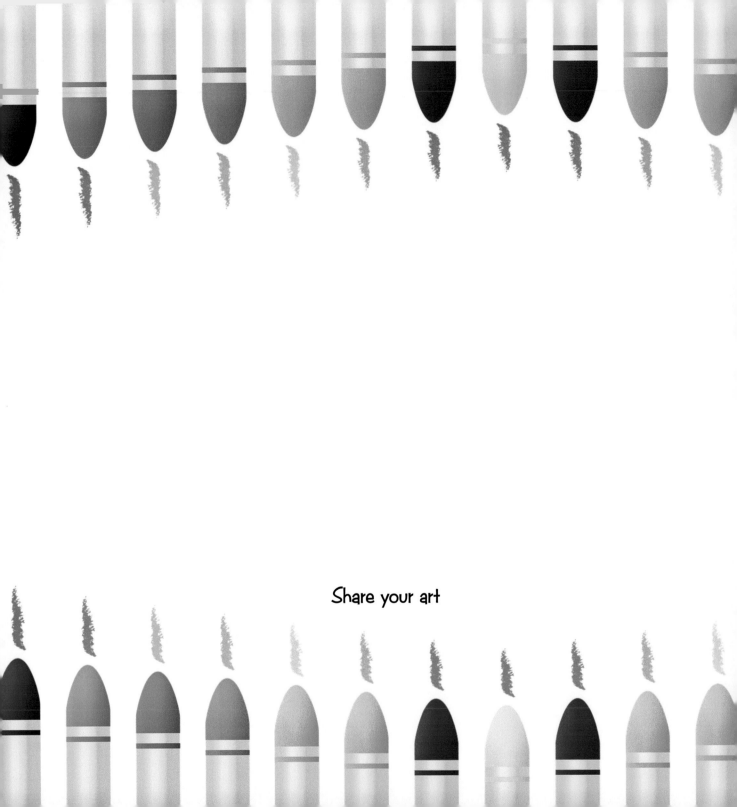

Share your art

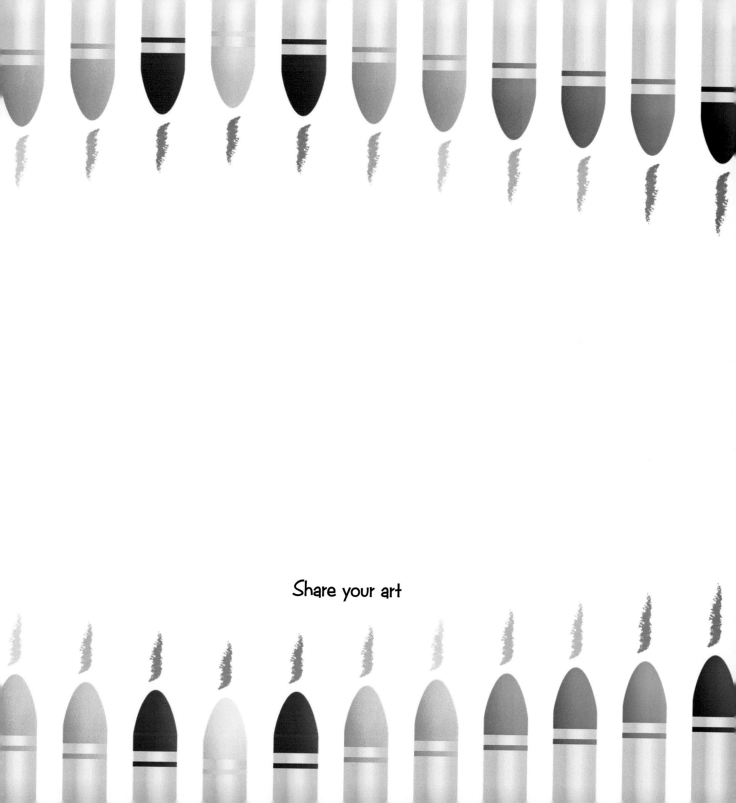

Share your art

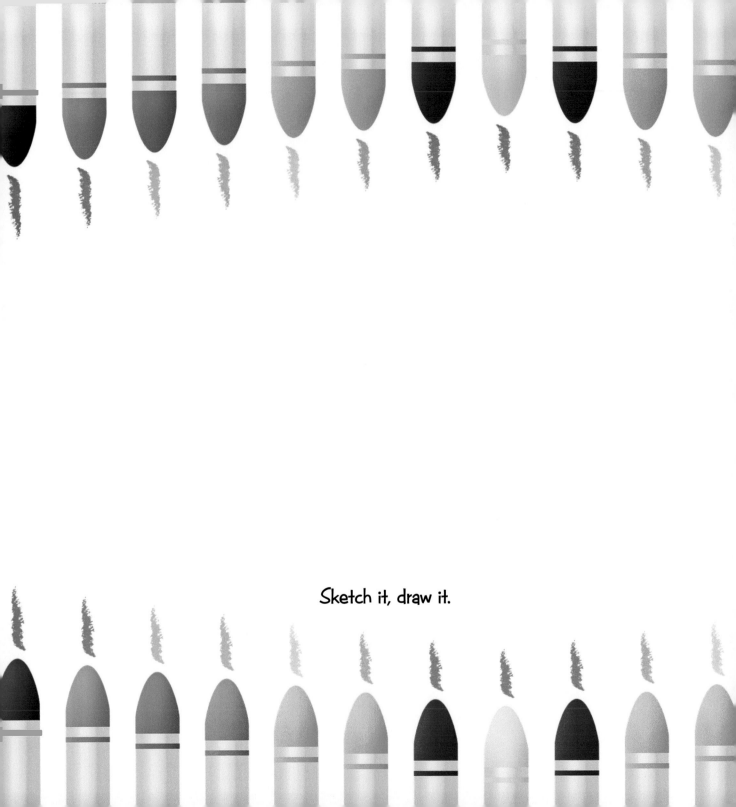

Sketch it, draw it.

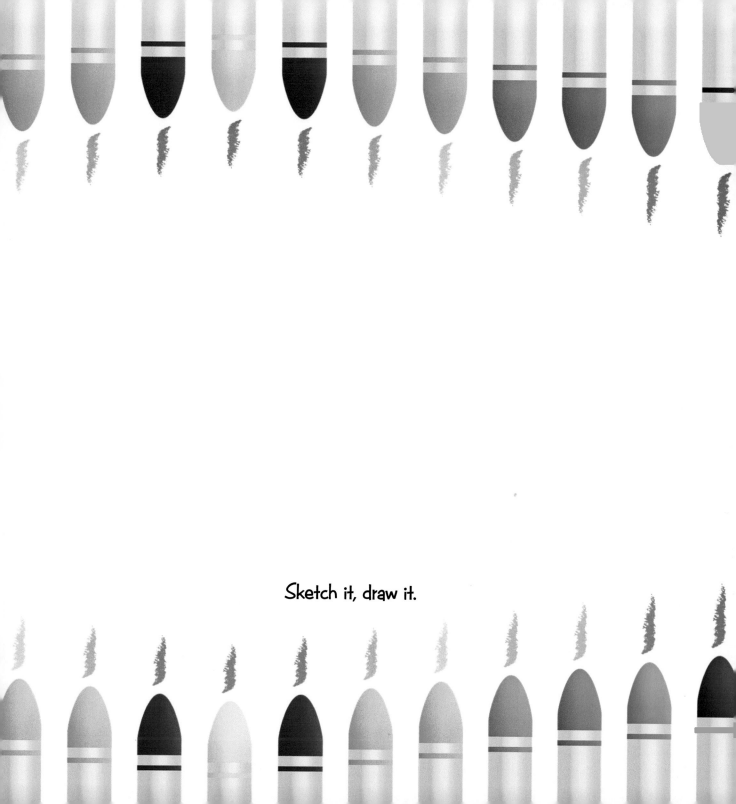

Sketch it, draw it.

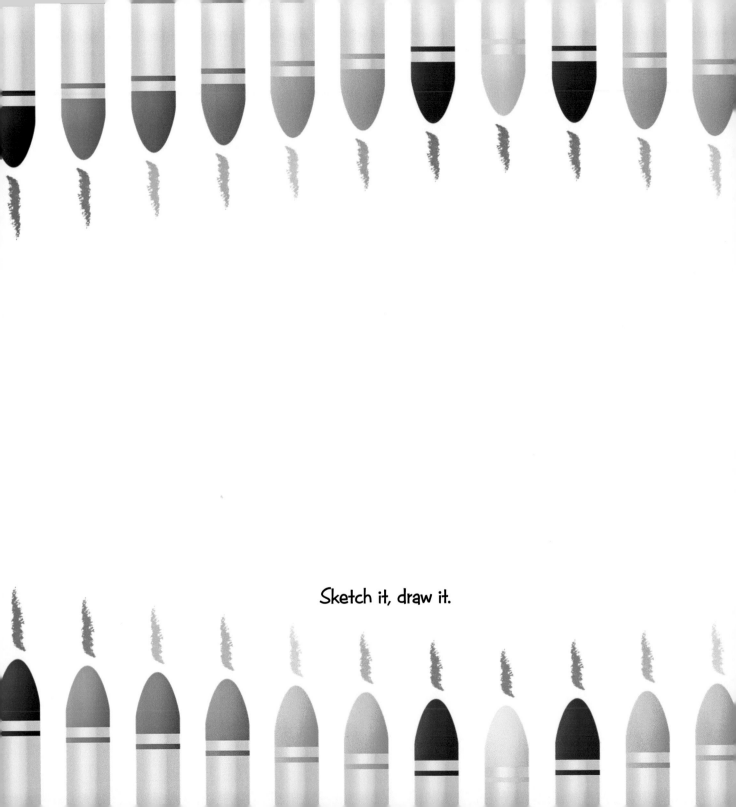

Sketch it, draw it.

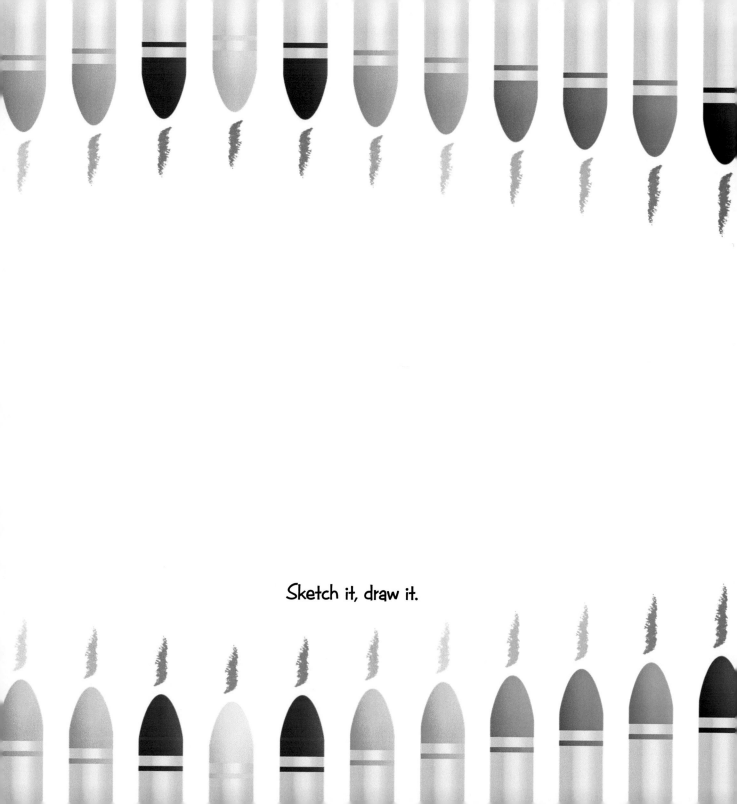

Sketch it, draw it.

Sketch to express.

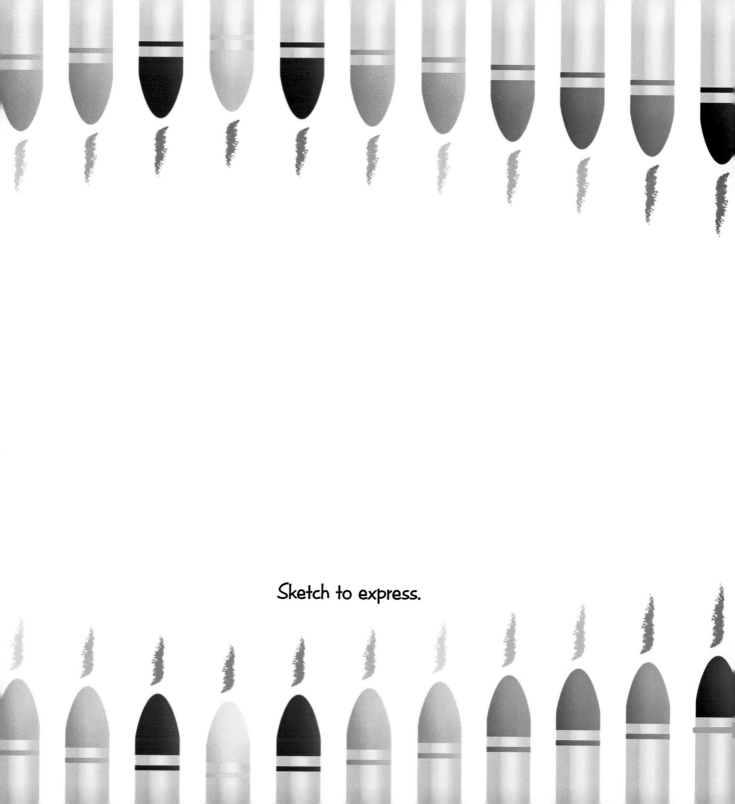

Sketch to express.

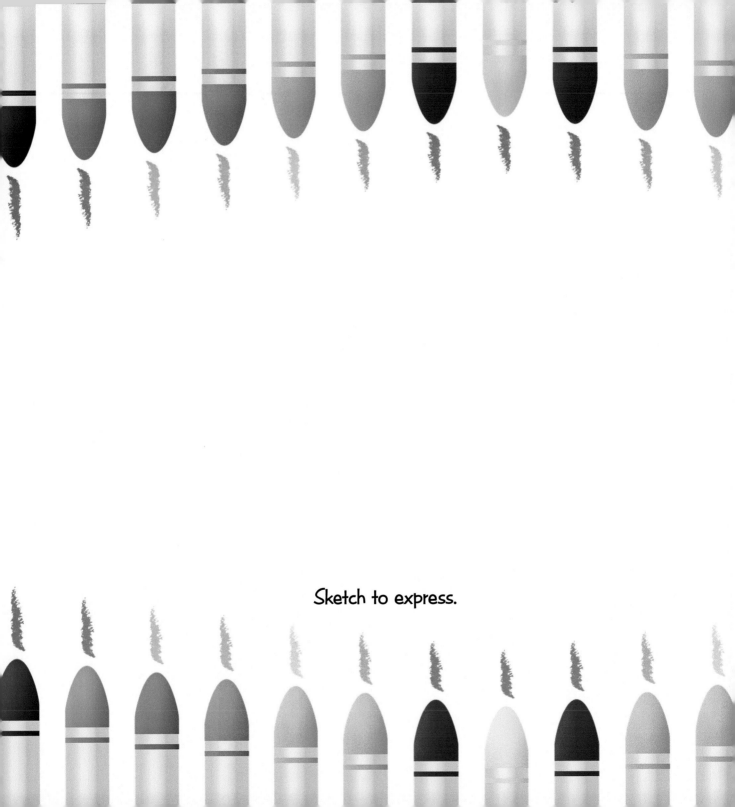

Sketch to express.

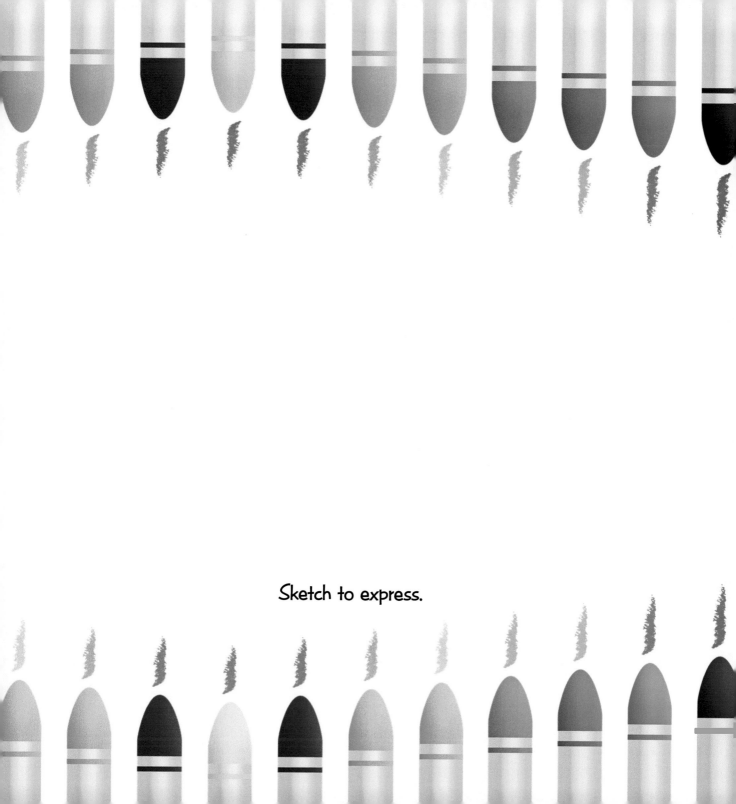

Sketch to express.

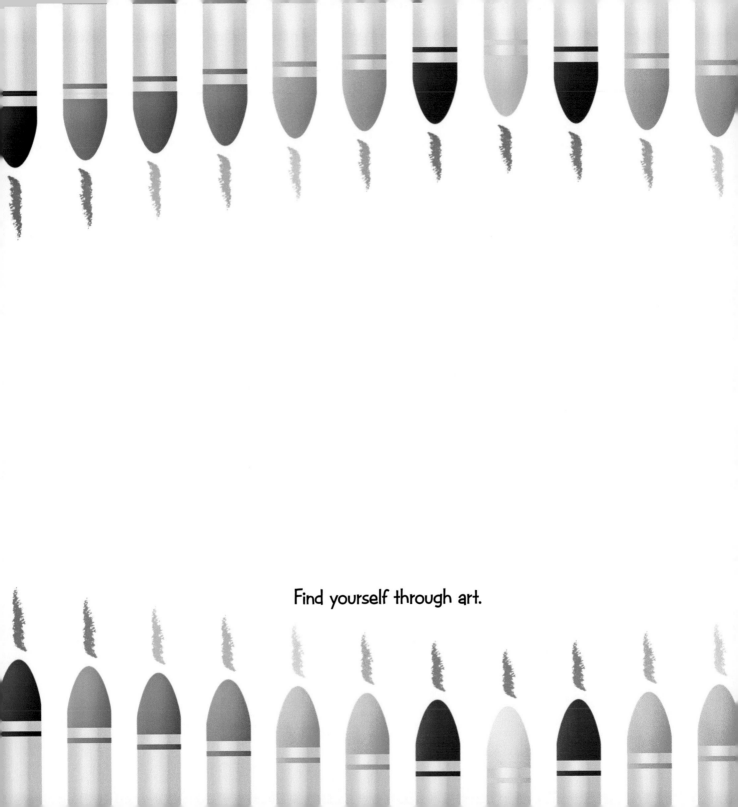

Find yourself through art.

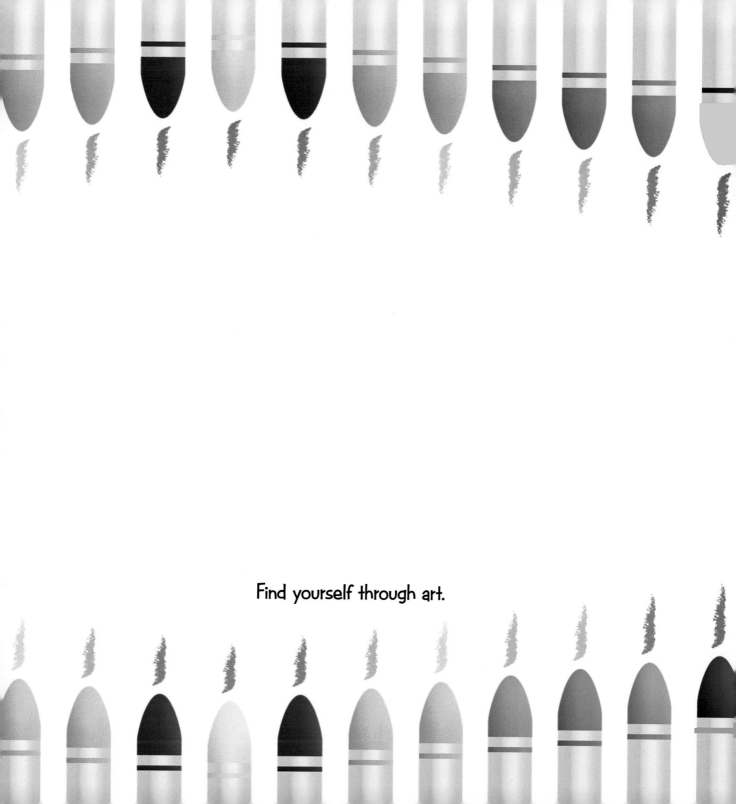

Find yourself through art.

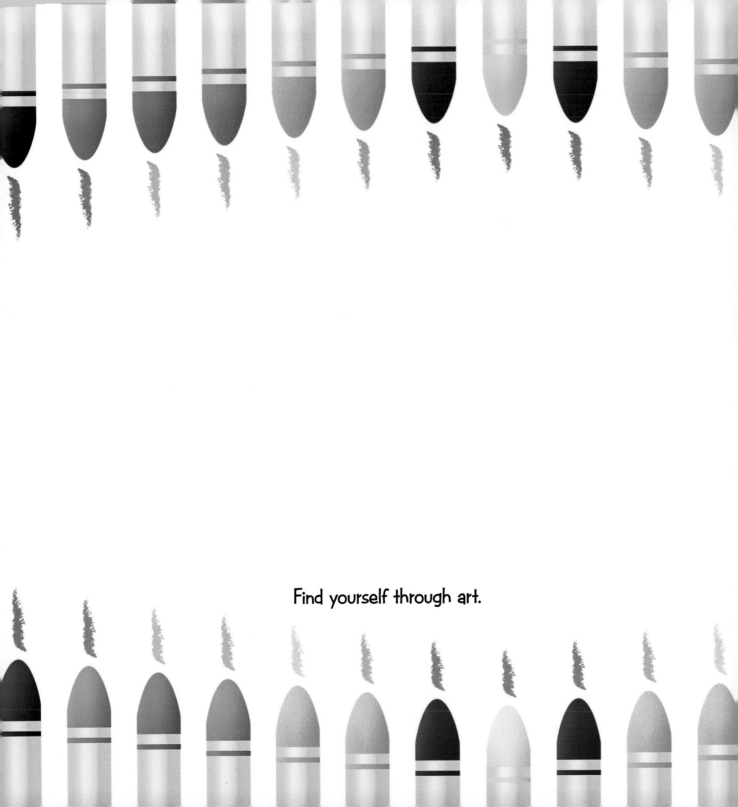

Find yourself through art.

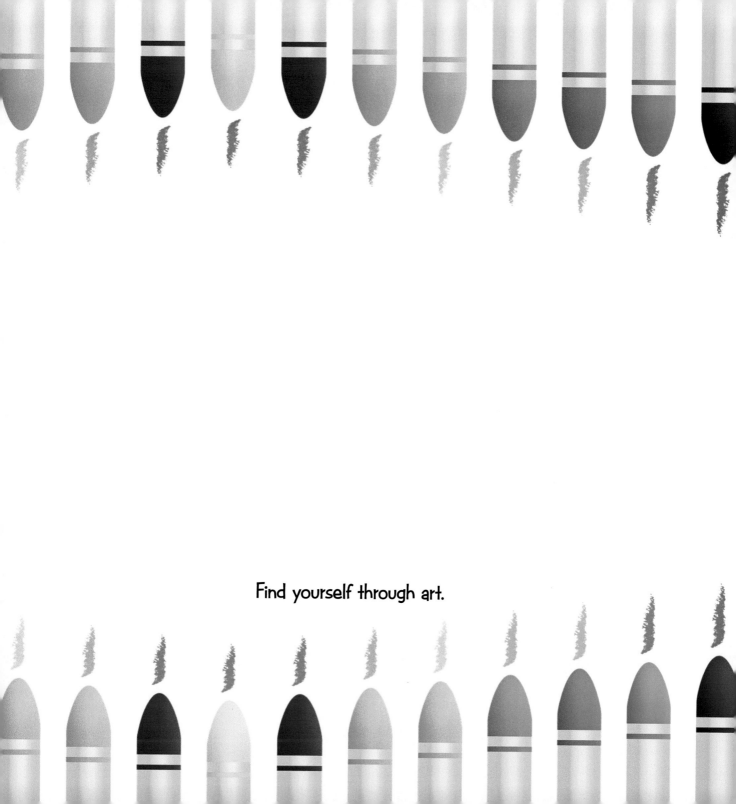

Find yourself through art.

Printed in the United States
By Bookmasters